THE WAY OF LOVE

A PRACTICAL GUIDE
TO FOLLOWING JESUS

D1738723

Scott Gunn

THE WAY OF LOVE

A PRACTICAL GUIDE
TO FOLLOWING JESUS

Scott Gunn

With
Brendan O'Sullivan-Hale, Linda Ryan,
Hill Liles, Sandra Montes, Richelle Thompson,
Lelanda Lee, and Miriam McKenney

Forward Movement
Cincinnati, Ohio

©2020 Forward Movement, Second Printing

ISBN: 978-0-88028-486-8

Printed in the USA

Forward Movement
inspire disciples. empower evangelists.

TABLE OF CONTENTS

FOREWORD

It's probably not an accident that most of Jesus'
teachings about love are uttered the closer he gets
to sacrificing his life for the sake of others.

I give you a new commandment, that you love one another.

*By this everyone will know that you are my disciples, if you
have love for one another.*

As the Father has loved me, so have I loved you.

Jesus spoke all these words during the last supper,
according to the Gospel of John. Judas would soon
betray him. Peter would soon pretend to not know
him, and others would soon abandon Jesus. Secular
and religious forces would array against him as he
faced a future of false charges, torture, and execution.
Yet Jesus spoke of love.

Such love is not a mere sentiment but a real commitment to a way of life that is sacrificial and redemptive, a way that seeks the good of God and the well-being of others. This Way of Love is a game changer.

During Holy Week in Matthew's Gospel, Jesus has a conversation with a lawyer as he nears the decision to give his life. This interaction may well be one of the most stunning—and one of the most stunningly underestimated—passages in the whole Bible. The lawyer, for whatever reason, asks Jesus to name the most important law in the entire legal edifice of Moses. Jesus reaches back to Leviticus and Deuteronomy to identify two laws of Moses that answer the question.

> He said to him, "'You shall love the Lord your God with all your heart, and with all your soul, and with all your mind.' This is the greatest and first commandment. And a second is like it: 'You shall love your neighbor as yourself.'"
> —Matthew 22:37-39

Then the stunner. Jesus add these words: "On these two commandments hang all the law and the prophets." The English Standard Version translates it this way: "On these two commandments depend all the Law and the Prophets." The Message paraphrase of the Bible renders it this way: "These two commands are pegs; everything in God's Law and the Prophets hangs from them."

In other words, this is it. Love God. Love your neighbor. And while you're at it, love yourself. Everything that Moses taught, everything the prophets thundered forth about justice and righteousness and truth, everything written in the scriptures, everything in the tradition of religion, everything that claims to be of or about God must reflect love. Love is God's way of life because, as 1 John says, "God is love." God is the source and the origin of love. "Where true love is found, God himself is there," says the medieval hymn. To put it another way, if it's not about love, it's not about God. And if it truly is about love, it is about God. And that's a game changer when we dare to believe and live this truth.

My friend Charles Marsh, a professor at the University of Virginia, writes about this extraordinary love in his book *The Beloved Community: How Faith Shapes*

Social Justice from the Civil Rights Movement to Today. He proclaims that Jesus "founded the most revolutionary movement in human history; a movement built on the unconditional love of God for the world and the mandate to live that love."

My friend is right! Jesus founded a movement that is revolutionary when it is lived. Jesus—his teachings, his example, his very life—became the center of the lives of his followers. And his way of love became their way of life. Their lives were profoundly changed, and they helped God change the world for the good in their time. What was true for them in the first century is true for us in the twenty-first!

A few years ago, a group of Episcopalians gathered in Atlanta to help me think about how to encourage all of us as the church to be the modern iteration of the Jesus Movement.

We soon realized that we didn't have to invent something new. The deep roots of Judaism and Christianity offer rich and time-tested spiritual practices and disciplines, ways of prayer, meditation, study, hospitality, and witness. For centuries, these practices have helped to draw those who engaged them into a loving, liberating, and life-giving relationship with God and into loving, liberating, and life-giving relationships with others and with God's world. The folks we speak of as saints consistently engaged these spiritual practices, which nourished in them a Jesus-centered life of love and witness.

We wondered: What would happen if we asked every Episcopalian to adopt these practices for a Jesus-centered life? How would God, through us, change lives and the world?

The group developed the concept of the Way of Love. But to be certain, it is not a program, done once and put away on a shelf. The Way of Love is a set of ancient spiritual practices to help every Episcopalian develop a Jesus-centered rule of life.

The words—Turn! Learn! Pray! Worship! Bless! Go! Rest!—emerged as verbs that captured the spirit of this way. Go and make disciples! Go and proclaim good news! Go and be my witnesses in Jerusalem,

Judaea, in Samaria, in first-century Galilee and in
the twenty-first century world! Go! And then Rest.
As the old hymn says:

O Sabbath rest of Galilee!
O calm of hills above,
Where Jesus knelt to share with Thee,
The silence of eternity,
Interpreted by love.

This book offers a guide to embarking on the Way of
Love. It is full of practical advice for how to embrace
the seven Way of Love spiritual practices with an
approach that is authentic and personal. My prayer
is that this book will help you and me and all of us to
throw our very lives into the hands of Jesus, such that
his way of love becomes our way of life, and his life
becomes ours.

God love you. God bless you. And may God hold us all
in those almighty hands of love.

Michael B. Curry
XXVII Presiding Bishop
The Episcopal Church

INTRODUCTION

Not long ago, Bishop Michael Curry, presiding bishop of the Episcopal Church, gathered a small group to meet with him for two days in Atlanta. He had spent the last couple of years challenging his church to claim the mantle of the Episcopal branch of the Jesus Movement. It was time to think about how to build on that challenging and inviting message.

There were about a dozen of us in total, and we shared an invigorating conversation steeped in prayer. It didn't take long for a consensus to build among the group that the next step should be a focus on spiritual practices. At that Atlanta meeting, our small group quickly reached consensus that regular worship, scripture study, daily prayer, service of others, and evangelism would be key practices. Bishop Curry's staff did a brilliant job of taking our skeleton and adding both depth and accessibility to a bold initiative called the Way of Love.

As Bishop Curry's invitation to spiritual practices, the Way of Love uses seven key verbs: Turn. Learn. Pray. Worship. Bless. Go. Rest. This book is an exploration of what these verbs mean in the context of our life of faith. More importantly, I hope it is a practical and encouraging guide to begin or deepen your own spiritual practices as a follower of Jesus.

I am excited about the Way of Love and its potential to transform the world one life at a time. It is completely approachable and yet so deep we could spend a lifetime exploring its expanse. The Way of Love does not require fancy programs or big budgets. We who follow Jesus need only to make the commitment to live our lives in ways that draw us ever deeper into becoming more Christlike. To follow Jesus is to make extraordinary commitments. We are to love God with our whole being. We are to love our neighbors as ourselves. We are to love others as Jesus has loved us, even taking up our own cross.

But this life of faith is far from burdensome. To follow Jesus is to know the hope, mercy, and grace he offered the world and that he offers each one of us. The cross is a sign of Christ's love for us, and the empty tomb of Easter morning is a sign of God's power over evil and death.

Following Jesus is easier said than done, and that's why we need to find a way to live this cross-shaped life. The Way of Love invites us to deep disciplines that remind us daily of God's great love for us and calls us to share that love with a world in need of hope. The Way of Love practices are as simple as daily prayer with God and spending some time with God's word in the Bible.

How to use this book

You can certainly pick up this book and move through it on your own. Each chapter offers clear explanations of the seven steps of the Way of Love as well as practical ways you might begin or further enrich your journey. At the end of each chapter, you'll find reflection questions to ponder before continuing on to the next practice. There is also space to make notes.

Please write in this book (unless you got it from the library!). In the final chapter, you'll have a chance to review what you've written and read in previous chapters and craft a rule of life to help you pursue the Way of Love.

This book also works well for group study or a formation class. The reflection questions serve as catalysts for small-group conversation. The group or class leader can teach each step over seven sessions or move more quickly in the context of a parish retreat or workshop day. Perhaps leaders will share their own stories to supplement or even replace the stories shared here. Individuals can make notes in the book and create a personalized rule of life, or the group might consider a collective rule of life for their time together.

The biblical readings referenced throughout the book are included in the appendix to make it easier to read the full narrative. If you'd like to look up the verses in your own Bible, you can do that as well. We used the New Revised Standard Version of the Bible and *The Book of Common Prayer* for psalm and liturgy quotations.

We also gathered some suggested resources for
further exploration and listed them in the back
of this book. You can also find many other Way of
Love resources at the Forward Movement website
(forwardmovement.org) or the Episcopal Church
website (episcopalchurch.org/wayoflove).

Gratitude

The gathering in Atlanta was a spiritual high point
for me. I am grateful to Michael Curry for the
invitation to be part of the group. He was joined by
key members of his staff, including Stephanie Spellers,
Michael Hunn, and Chuck Robertson. Bill Lupfer
hosted the conversation. Our discernment group was
Mariann Budde, Megan Castellan, Courtney Cowart,
Frank Logue, Tricia Lyons, Jesús Reyes, Rob Wright,
Dwight Zscheile, and me. I am thankful for the seven
inspiring people who answered the call to offer
personal reflections for this volume. The manuscript
was much improved because of helpful feedback
I received on an early draft from Steve Pankey,
Melody Shobe, and Adam Trambley. Rachel Jones
and Richelle Thompson made my prose better with

their editorial skill, and Lexi Caoili created a lovely design. Everything that Forward Movement offers is the fruit of our whole staff, and I could list every staff person as having made a contribution to this volume. I am blessed to serve with such skilled and passionate workers. Of course, above all, I am grateful for the grace upon grace bestowed upon us and the world in the saving work of Jesus Christ.

Scott Gunn
Easter Day 2020
Cincinnati, Ohio

CHAPTER 1

TURN

Turning—the first and most basic spiritual practice—is what makes the Christian life possible. If I believe everything about my life and the world is just fine, I can keep on going in the direction I'm headed. But once I realize everything is not all right with me or the world, I also realize I need to change direction—toward God and away from my self-centered way.

Turn is a gentler way to talk about a harder churchy concept: repentance. One of the key concepts in Jesus' message, repentance comes from the Greek word *metanoia*. It means "change of mind." This isn't in a flip way, like when I decide to have pancakes instead of waffles. *Metanoia* means a deeper transformation, a completely new way of thinking.

This gets to the heart of the gospel. Matthew's Gospel says that the very first public teaching of Jesus is about turning. "From that time Jesus began to proclaim, saying, 'Repent, for the kingdom of heaven has come near'" (Matthew 4:17).

Turning is not a one-and-done endeavor. While some Christians say we simply accept Jesus as Lord and Savior and then we're finished with the turning business, Anglican Christianity understands turning as something we do in big and in small ways every day. Each time we turn, we admit we were going the wrong way and must head in a new direction.

Though turning must be a part of our journey day-in, day-out, there is one big turn that we make. The Christian life begins in the baptismal font. There, we are reborn spiritually, cleansed from our sins, and grafted into Christ's body, the church. *The Book of Common Prayer* makes it clear that those to be baptized are turning. "Do you turn to Jesus Christ and accept him as your Savior?" (p. 302).

At baptism, we reject Satan and his wickedness, the evil powers of this world, and the sinful desires that draw us from the love of God. We turn toward Jesus Christ, accepting him as our savior and trusting in his grace and love. We promise to follow Jesus and obey him as our Lord. When we are faithful in our promise to follow Jesus, we become willing and ready to keep turning back to him each time we go off course.

Turning in big and small ways

How do we turn? How can we manage to get this right? Good news, friends! We aren't alone, and we don't have to get it right every time. In fact, we'll mess up far more often than we manage to do the right thing.

When I realized God was calling me to leave behind a rewarding career in technology to serve as a priest, I had to turn. That was a big turn. When I do something dumb and hurt a friend's feelings, when I decide to apologize and seek reconciliation, that's a medium change. When driving in Boston not long ago, it occurred to me that letting someone cut in front of me was a kind of generosity that might be good for my soul. That was an example of just turning my head and heart ever so slightly and seeing things in a new way, a small turn.

One of my favorite baptismal promises is helpful in thinking about turning. The celebrant asks, "Will you persevere in resisting evil, and, *whenever* you fall into sin, repent and return to the Lord?" And we reply, "I will, with God's help." I love this promise because it assures me that I can only do these things with God's help. And it assumes that I will fall into sin: it's not *if* I fall into sin but *whenever* I fall into sin.

We don't have to get life's decisions right all the time. We just have to try. Grace comes alongside us when we try—and helps us recognize that people around us are trying too. And in all our efforts to try to turn, God is our abiding companion and guide.

The burning bush

The story of Moses is amazing, epic even. (Exodus 3 has the whole story, and we've included it in the appendix for you to enjoy. Or you can look it up in your own Bible. But you should read it. It's great.) Early in Moses' story is a moment that is both

ordinary and mind-bogglingly supernatural. One day
Moses is minding his own business, tending his sheep.
As he walks along, he sees a burning bush. Nothing in
the text suggests Moses knows *why* the bush is burning.

Imagine the scene. Moses is busily taking care of his
sheep, and he probably has a long to-do list running
through his head—grazing, watering, safety, shady
spot for a nap. The normal thing to do would be to
make note of the bush and keep walking to the next
grassy spot or water well. But that's not what Moses
does. You can almost hear him, "Huh, that's weird. I
guess I'll go check it out." What Moses actually says,
according to Exodus, is, "I must turn aside and look at
this great sight and see why the bush is not burned up."

Moses turns.

We shouldn't take this for granted. Moses doesn't
know he is about to speak with the living and true
God. Moses has concrete, definite things to do—and a
plan for doing them. Despite all that, he turns.

When Moses walks over to the burning bush, God
speaks to him. God assures Moses that the suffering
of the Hebrews has been seen and that God will work

to liberate them. God tells Moses that he will soon challenge Pharaoh and lead the people to freedom in the promised land. All this because Moses turned.

Imagine if Moses had stuck to his plan. The sheep would have gotten where they needed to go a bit sooner. But God's plan of salvation wouldn't have worked out the same way. We don't know how the story would be different—and we don't have to speculate because Moses made the choice to turn. Our ancestors' freedom rested on Moses' simple decision to turn aside from his own plans, to be drawn toward God.

The turning couldn't have been simpler—literally a few steps down a well-worn path. But the consequences couldn't have been more significant.

My own turning

Not long after we moved to Cincinnati, my spouse and I were out doing errands and walking around downtown. I'm the goal-tracker in our relationship, so I was probably reminding Sherilyn that we needed to hurry up.

Along the way, we passed a man holding a sign asking for food. I made eye contact and spoke to him, thinking that was a kind thing to do. But Sherilyn stopped, turned aside from our journey and our orderly list of tasks, and asked the man if we could buy him lunch.

We were standing near a Mexican fast food place, and as we walked toward the restaurant, I was grateful we were feeding a hungry person. I was also hoping it wouldn't take too long, but God had other plans—the line was out the door. While we waited in line, we had little choice but to talk with our guest. We shared names and talked about downtown Cincinnati. He told us a bit about his story, and we told him a bit about ours. When it was time to order, we offered to buy him whatever he wanted. He only wanted a burrito.

He thanked us more profusely than we deserved... certainly more than I deserved. It wasn't hard to do the right thing. It took ten minutes and cost a few dollars. Later that day, I thought about our encounter. I realized—and I know this is going to sound hokey, but stick with me—we bought Jesus a burrito. In Matthew 25, Jesus says that when we feed the hungry, clothe the naked, visit prisoners, welcome strangers, and the like, we are doing these things for Christ himself. We wouldn't have met this man if Sherilyn hadn't turned aside. If it had been up to me, we would have missed out on feeding a hungry person. I am sure we met Jesus on the sidewalk because of a simple turn.

PERSONAL REFLECTION: TURN

When I was baptized in my early twenties as a college senior, sin didn't mean much to me. For one thing, an unseemly emphasis on sin was why I had deliberately chosen not to join several churches. For another, the end of apartheid in South Africa and the collapse of European communism made me believe humanity might have arrived at a new era of goodness. Why did I need a robust theology of sin when so much of what I considered systematic sin was becoming history too?

The years between that young man and the less-young man I am now have lent some maturity and given me a greater willingness to examine my actions and motivations. These two hallmarks of adulthood have led me to understand how naive I was.

When making choices about money or my career, I've had—and often chosen—the great luxury to do whatever seemed the best thing for me, never minding whether it was actually the right thing to do. This has resulted in sometimes being a neglectful friend and an inattentive spouse, despite my best intentions. When I think about my material comfort when so many are in need, I soothe myself with the fiction that there's really nothing I can do to make things different...or better.

This state of the soul—mine, and probably yours and most of the other people we know—is as old as Paul's plaintive musing, "For I do not do the good I want, but the evil I do not want is what I do. Wretched man that I am! Who will rescue me from this body of death?" (Romans 7:19, 24).

Jesus promises us that when we stop deceiving ourselves about our ability to overcome sin and turn to follow him, we will find forgiveness and grace.

I made that turn at my baptism, not realizing I would need to make it over and over again for a lifetime. By gathering regularly with a group to pray, worship, study and do the kinds of loving service that Jesus taught, I am more aware of the turns and more willing and able to make them. These disciplines don't shield us from failure, but they do bind our wandering hearts to Christ so that when we stray, it is easier to turn back to him—our companion in the Way of Love.

—*Brendan O'Sullivan-Hale*

Brendan O'Sullivan-Hale is canon to the ordinary for administration and evangelism in the Episcopal Diocese of Indianapolis, where he manages finances and operations and supports lay and clergy leaders in developing creative strategies to observe how God is acting in the communities they serve and responding faithfully with the good news of Jesus Christ. He is a member of the Episcopal Church of All Saints, Indianapolis.

※ ※ ※

The real point of these stories about turning is that if we are so stubborn about sticking to our plans, we will miss encounters with Jesus Christ. Since that day outside of the Mexican fast food restaurant, I understand that what seems like a digression might be the most important thing I am called to do. Taking that turn, being willing to go off course or getting off-topic is one of the ways we find out what God is calling us to do, where to go, and how to be.

Think of examples of when you have turned. Recalling times when you have done the right thing or turned back toward God or even made a simple course correction feels good. We don't spend enough time in our culture talking about our spiritual successes. It feels like bragging, even though it isn't—it is sharing good news. We need to spend time telling each other our turning stories. Sharing these stories will help us see that turning is not nearly as complicated as we make it.

Which way to turn?

How do we know which way to go? How can we be sure we're turning toward Jesus and not away from him? I think most of the time, these choices and turns are pretty clear. And when they are not, we have a variety of tools to help us see more clearly the will of God. We can study the scriptures so that we might know the mind of Christ in God's word. We can spend time in a church community so that we have the aid of other pilgrims along the way. We can pray, opening our hearts and eyes in the trust that God will show us the way.

We won't get it right all the time. We will fail to turn. We will fall in our turning. We will turn the wrong direction. But the very, very Good News of God in Jesus Christ is that we aren't turning so that we can finally deserve God's love. God loves us more than we can ask or imagine. On the cross, Jesus Christ accomplished our salvation. On Easter morning, God the Father raised Jesus Christ from the dead, showing that God's love is stronger than death or any evil in the world. And Jesus promises that the Holy Spirit will abide with us, leading us into all truth.

We do not turn to earn God's love—we turn in order to give thanks and enjoy God's vast love for us. Jesus came to save sinners and his greatest desire is that we be free from the tyranny of sin and death. In faith, we turn to him again and again, so that we might know and enjoy the eternal life he has promised.

How do we turn?

Your own journey will be different from anyone else's, so there's no one-size-fits-all approach. Nevertheless, there are some common approaches to turning that can help us in our journey.

- If you are not already baptized, speak with your priest and ask about preparing for baptism. This might be the most important turn for someone who wants to follow Jesus.

- Set aside (more) intentional time for daily prayer and study of scripture in your life.

- Perhaps you have an estranged friend with whom you might practice reconciliation. Maybe you can be extravagantly generous with someone in great need who cannot pay you back for what you offer. Pick something that is an example of clearly turning toward Jesus and give it a try.

- Nurture spiritual friendships. It's important to have spiritual friendships to share your highs and lows and to be part of a church community.

- Commit to regular worship. Offering our thanks and praise—and being fed by the sacraments— keeps us heading in the right direction and nourishes us for the journey.

Turning usually feels pretty good. Don't be ashamed of that. This doesn't mean you are being prideful. The Christian life is meant to be deeply joyful. Share your joy with a friend or someone in your church. Encourage other people on their journey.

FOR REFLECTION

1. When is a time you turned in a way that helped you grow in your faith?

2. What keeps you from turning more readily?

3. What might you do to turn in new ways, more often?

WRITE IT DOWN

Which of the approaches for turning appeal to you?
Write down some ideas for how you might live into
this approach. Be specific and realistic for where you
are now. For instance, if you decide to devote more
time to prayer and Bible study, name the time, place,
and frequency that you can really do this.

PRAY

Almighty God, help me reject those things that keep me from your ways, and give me strength and courage to turn to follow your life-giving son, Jesus Christ. *Amen*.

CHAPTER 2

LEARN

Each year, I look forward to the Sunday nearest November 16. The reason for my anticipation is kind of funny: I love the prayer (collect) assigned for that day. It reads like this:

Blessed Lord, who caused all holy Scriptures to be written for our learning: Grant us so to hear them, read, mark, learn, and inwardly digest them, that we may embrace and ever hold fast the blessed hope of everlasting life, which you have given us in our Savior Jesus Christ; who lives and reigns with you and the Holy Spirit, one God, for ever and ever. Amen. *(The Book of Common Prayer,* p. 236)

Thomas Cranmer wrote this prayer for the 1549 *Book of Common Prayer*, and it is a masterpiece of language. But that's not why I love it. I love this prayer because it celebrates the importance of holy scripture, reminding us why the Bible matters. I love how the prayer reminds us that the scriptures are written for our learning—to teach us about God revealed as Father, Son, and Holy Spirit. I love that we're told to take notes in our Bibles (to mark them up…like with a pen or pencil or highlighter). We're told to inwardly digest them—to learn them so well that the scriptures become a part of who we are.

Cranmer wrote this collect in the sixteenth century as the Bible was becoming more accessible to more people. While it's not entirely true to say that the Bible had been kept away from lay people, learning the scriptures by reading the Bible was not widely encouraged prior to the reformations of Cranmer's time.

Ironically, we live once again in an era when people who come to church may not know much—or any—scripture. While we have the freedom to read the Bible as much as we want, many studies show that Bible reading is not widely practiced. Why should we learn from the scriptures? Does it matter?

I think there are at least two methods we should practice when it comes to studying and learning the scriptures. We might call them digesting "facts" and discerning "meaning."

Let's imagine a person learning family history. When I was growing up, I learned about my aunts and uncles, other ancestors, and family lore. These are all facts. Perhaps someone reminded me that when I was young, my grandmother cooked a particular food for me one holiday. This is a fact, but it becomes part of a broader pattern. My grandmother cooked this favorite food because she loved me. Indeed, learning about our families and their stories teaches us both facts as well as identity and meaning. I am loved. I am part of a wider family. When I learn about my family, I understand the fact that my grandmother cooked a particular food because she loved me. The cooking *meant something*. So it is with the Bible.

Facts and meaning in the Bible

Some of what we learn about in the Bible are simple facts. Mary was Jesus' mother. Elizabeth was John the Baptist's mother. Herod was the king. Most of the stories of Jesus' life took place in Galilee or Jerusalem. Jesus died on a cross. And so on.

There is also the meaning of those stories, the deep meaning that extends beyond the bare facts. When I read the totality of Jesus' life, I see how much God the Father loves me—that God's own son Jesus Christ entered our world. I learn that God loves me so much that the Holy Spirit still abides with us today.

I am loved. I am part of a breathtakingly vast story.

It took me a long time to see the Bible this way. I was a priest before I really understood how important the Bible is to us and how much it can change us. When I was ordained, I had an undergraduate degree in religion and two graduate degrees in theology. I had studied biblical Hebrew. I thought I was pretty competent in the scriptures. My understanding of the Bible's meaning shifted and grew when the second congregation I served decided to read the whole Bible together.

We started our year by reading the Old and New Testaments in their entirety—out loud. We read the Bible for all ages in our Sunday morning classes.

We offered a midweek course. The experience was amazing. Lives transformed as we learned the facts of the Bible and as we learned about our own identity and meaning as God's beloved, all of us a part of a vast sweeping story.

This encounter with the scriptures changed me. I realized I had been missing the point. I felt like I had gone to an art museum to look at a Monet painting. As I stood before the painting, I stared closely at various flowers and points of light. I studied the brush strokes and paint colors. I knew about the garden at Giverny where Monet painted many of his works. But I had never done one obvious thing: backed up to gaze at the whole painting. I was so concerned with facts and details that I had never stepped back to see the wonders of the light and colors, the shadows and the textures—I had never seen what it *meant*.

When I read the Bible with fellow travelers, I stepped back and gazed on the whole gorgeous panorama for the first time. I had focused on the facts, the brainy bits easily cataloged. In the community of that congregation, though, I stepped back to see the wider view. Suddenly, in a breathtaking way, I saw the vastness of God's love for us revealed in the scriptures from the moment of creation until the end of history. I saw the Bible as the story of God's great love and found my place in the midst of it.

We can always learn something—all of us, no matter how old or smart or well-read we are. Priests—and lay folk—are still learning all the time, or at least we should be. The task of learning isn't just for new Christians: it's for all of us. There's no shame in not knowing something. There is only the good of learning, of moving along—of finding and applying both facts and meaning to our lives.

PERSONAL REFLECTION: LEARN

What can I learn today?

I don't say that to myself every morning when I first awaken, but subconsciously I look throughout the day for something new to think about, understand, or apply to the world outside my head. Sometimes I learn from the TV or the radio, from a sermon, class discussion, or even something said in passing. At other times, learning comes from a passage I read in a book or other visual presentation.

I use videos to help me understand how to do new tasks like minor repairs around the house. I might pick up a sheet of music and try a new piano piece or read a book about a spiritual practice. Some endeavors are successful, and some are not. Still, each one gives me a different perspective to consider.

Working alongside others helps me learn about community, diversity, and communication. Usually, this kind of formation takes place at my job, in my neighborhood, or with folks at my church. It can also take place in groups like Education for Ministry (EfM). EfM is a ministry of the School of Theology at the University of the South that brings together study of the scriptures, church history, and theology. This four-year course is available to anyone interested in such topics. It can profoundly open the eyes and heart to the vast wealth of wisdom and knowledge from the Bible as well as to the ideas and wrestlings of some of the giants of faith. This program helps participants see that ministry is not just for the ordained but the laity as well.

EfM taught me to use theological reflection, a way of looking at a range of things through spiritual lenses and finding God in unexpected places. Discussion of sensitive cultural, environmental, or moral issues can take place anywhere, but within the context of EfM, I can focus on the presence of God in such conversations. EfM has been an excellent way for me to engage and grow my faith through the study of scripture as well as the development of religion and tradition over the history of humankind.

I wonder what I will learn tomorrow.

—*Linda Ryan*

Linda Ryan lives in Arizona but will always consider Virginia home. She has been a weekly contributor to Speaking to the Soul *for Episcopal Café. She is also an online mentor for Education for Ministry. Linda keeps the blog Jerichosdaughter@blogspot.com.*

❋ ❋ ❋

Learning leads to growth

Learning about our faith—especially by engaging the scriptures but also by participating in the liturgy and theological traditions—helps us grow. RenewalWorks, a ministry of Forward Movement, has done a great deal of work in studying the spectrum of spiritual growth in the Episcopal Church. From that research, we know that people who have particular beliefs are more likely to grow in spiritual maturity.

The doctrine of grace is a wonderful illustration of this mode of learning. Grace is something that we need to be taught because it's countercultural. Grace is the free gift of God's love, the love God has for all people. God loves me, and there is nothing I can do to earn more of God's love. There is also nothing I can do to cause God to stop loving me. And the same is true for everyone else. God loves the virtuous person who seems to do everything right. God loves the seemingly messed-up person who is always getting into trouble. God loves the person who has been on every church committee for thirty years just the same amount as God loves the person who has stepped into a church for the first time, unsure of what to expect or hope for.

As we begin to understand the depth of God's love for us, we learn to love ourselves and others in more vital and vibrant ways. When I encounter people for whom it is difficult for me to love, the Holy Spirit reminds me that God's grace most certainly includes this difficult-for-me person. The doctrine of God's grace, if I learn it, can equip me on my own journey as a follower of Jesus.

How do we learn?

There is no one right or wrong way to learn, and odds are you have some methods that work for you. Here are a few examples of ways to engage scriptures—to learn more about the story of God and our place in it—and I encourage you to choose what works for you.

Read the Bible. Dive into the wondrous story of the Bible and change your life! You could pick up a Bible and just start reading, but I wouldn't recommend that for your first time through. Many people struggle if they start at the beginning of Genesis and try to read the whole Bible straight through like a regular book.

Maybe read one of the four gospels (Matthew, Mark, Luke, or John). Or read the psalms. Or read the page-turning action starting at the beginning of 1 Samuel (featuring the stories of Saul, David, Goliath, and so on). Whatever you do, just try reading some of the Bible. When you run into something you don't understand, look it up or ask a priest or a friend who has spent time with the scriptures.

If your church has one, join a Bible study with other people. I always learn a lot when I read the Bible with others, and you might too. If your church doesn't have a Bible study, visit with your priest or vestry member to see about starting one.

Try a Daily Devotion. *Forward Day by Day* is an approachable and time-tested daily devotion, available in print or on your favorite digital device or for free online. Each day offers a snippet of scripture along with a meditation on what you've read, a practical action step, and a place in the world for which to pray.

Join a Class. Many congregations offer courses in faith formation. These might meet on Sunday mornings, or they might be offered in the middle of the week. Topics will likely vary from scripture to history to contemporary affairs to theology. If your congregation doesn't have formation classes, try an online course.

Read Books. There are countless books about our faith to suit every interest and level of experience. Odds are a friend or a clergy person would be happy to recommend a good book to you—or several. We've also included a short, suggested reading list in the back of this book.

Learning changes us

Most of us understand that learning is essential as we move through life. We take our car to a mechanic who is well trained. We learn to cook, adapting recipes when we don't have all the listed ingredients. We navigate relationships in an adult way, not treating friends like we might have done as young children. Our faith is no different.

We want to be taught by someone who is well trained. We want to understand the spiritual journey and how to adapt to the changing circumstances of my life. We want to be able to respond to the inevitable struggles and trials of life in a reasonable and well-considered way, not the way we did as children.

Learning—deeply engaging and responding to scripture—will absolutely change our lives. We need to learn—to read, mark, and inwardly digest—not just the facts and particular stories but also the bigger picture of identity and meaning.

By reading this book, you are already showing a desire to learn. As you try to live out the other six practices of the Way of Love, you will discover that learning supports the other practices. Whatever you do, learning is possible—and the Holy Spirit is waiting to lead you.

FOR REFLECTION

1. When is a time you learned in a way that helped you grow in your faith?

2. What keeps you from learning?

3. What might you do to learn in new ways,
   more often?

WRITE IT DOWN

Which of the approaches for learning appeal to you?
Write down a plan for how you might live into this
approach. Be specific and realistic for where you are
now. For instance, if you decide to commit to reading
and praying a daily devotional, name the time and place.

PRAY

Give me an inquiring mind, O God, and enable me
to know your wisdom and to learn your Way of Love.
Amen.

CHAPTER 3
PRAY

When I was a parish priest, more than one person stopped by my office and sheepishly admitted they weren't quite sure how to pray. Let me be the first to say: there's no shame in not knowing how to pray or not having developed your prayer life yet. Prayer is like every other skill—we have to learn how to do it. Prayer can most certainly be learned.

Like most skills, prayer gets easier with practice, and our comfort and skill in the practice of prayer develops over time. This applies to every aspect of prayer. Someone who has never knelt by the bedside to talk to God at the end of the day will probably find it awkward the first time. Go through the motions a few hundred times, and you're likely to find talking to God as natural as talking with your best friend. The first time someone asks you to pray before a meal in a room full of people, you might want to shrivel up. But after enough practice, it becomes easier—a joy even.

My point is that if prayer isn't coming naturally to you, you're not alone. And it gets better. Even Jesus' disciples in the Bible weren't quite sure how to pray, and they got to hang out with Jesus Christ himself!

In the Gospel according to Luke, Jesus' followers ask him about prayer. "Lord, teach us to pray," they say (Luke 11:1). Jesus proceeds to teach them what we now call the Lord's Prayer or the Our Father. Matthew tells the story from another angle, and the prayer Jesus says is likely familiar to us.

Our Father in heaven,
hallowed be your name.
Your kingdom come.
Your will be done,
on earth as it is in heaven.
Give us this day our daily bread.
And forgive us our debts,
as we also have forgiven our debtors.
And do not bring us to the time of trial,
but rescue us from the evil one. (Matthew 6:9b-13)

It is lovely and amazing that we still pray today using the same words and phrases Jesus taught his followers. Of course, Jesus didn't speak English, but the content of our beloved Lord's Prayer is very much in line with the way the gospels record this prayer.

We should also note the type of prayer. Through the Lord's Prayer, Jesus wants his followers to pray with reverence for God's holiness, hopeful for the coming of God's kingdom of justice and mercy. Jesus calls on his followers to surrender to God's will and not our own, with confidence that we will be given just enough to sustain us and not more. Jesus teaches us to ask for our own forgiveness but also that we might forgive others—and to ask for deliverance from struggles and from Satan.

Notice that in the Lord's Prayer, there's nothing about getting what I want. This model provided by Jesus doesn't invite me to pray for a better job or favors or for much of anything that benefits me materially. The Lord's Prayer is about the whole world, about *us* rather than *me*, and above all about God's will being done.

Growing in prayer

Over the course of our lives in Christ, we are meant to mature. Just as infants and adults need different things and act differently, new Christians and mature Christians need different things and act differently. Saint Paul alluded to this in his first letter to the church in Corinth: "I fed you with milk, not solid food, for you were not ready for solid food" (1 Corinthians 3:2a).

Forward Movement's RenewalWorks research tells us that there is an evolution of prayer practices as people become more mature in their faith. It often goes like this:

We start by praying to God and asking for things.
Then we learn to give thanks for those blessings we have.
Then we learn to praise God and to ask for the well-being
*   of others.*
Then, finally, we learn to ask God for guidance.

Where are you on this journey in your life of prayer? Would you like to grow in commitment as a follower of Jesus? If you are already thanking God regularly, try a prayer that praises God's goodness, power, mercy, and love. Remember, if it's hard at first, that's normal. But practice always makes things easier.

There is nothing wrong with praying to God with our hopes, wants and desires—or our hurts, dreams, and fears. The point of a maturing prayer life is not to cease one kind of prayer in order to take up another but rather to develop a rich prayer life that is for our own needs, for the needs of the world, and for guidance.

The same research that teaches us about prayer and growth in faith teaches us something else that is vital: disciples who are growing in faith pray daily.

PERSONAL REFLECTION: PRAY

I don't know when I started praying—it's always been part of my life. I pray before meals, when things are going badly and I need help, and when I want to help someone but don't know how to be helpful. I pray for things that I benefit from but also that other people will benefit from—like world peace. Sometimes I pray with my family at home, like when we pray Compline together at night or when we grieve the loss of someone or something we love.

Even though I started praying because my parents told me to, I pray now for my own reasons. To be honest, I think I first started praying on my own because the wishes I made when my clock read 7:11 weren't coming true. I prayed to God instead of making wishes. And it's been a better experience—much better. Praying helps me get better acquainted with God. It allows me to say all of the things I wish were happening or were true, and I can talk about my concerns for people or situations that I feel like God might need to pay special attention to.

The thing that I enjoy most about praying is that it gives me someone to talk to, even when I'm all alone or not allowed to talk like when it's past lights out at summer camp. And even when I am really mad, I can ask the Lord to help me forgive the person I'm mad at.

Praying isn't always easy. Sometimes my schedule is busy. Sometimes I just forget to pray. When I do pray, I try to make it as detailed as possible because I want God to know that I am praising the amazing work God has done, that I am so grateful for how big God is, and that I am spreading God's love to as many people as possible in my life and in the world.

The most surprising thing about prayer—and my favorite thing—that I have experienced is that prayer is a great stress reliever. When I get too tired because I've done too much or when people haven't treated me well and everything seems against me, I know that the Lord loves me and is always with me. God loves me the same as God loves every other person. I can always express feelings or opinions to God no matter what they are.

—Hill Liles

Hill Liles lives in Dallas, Texas, with his parents, sister, and pet dog. He enjoys playing the piano, volunteering at the local animal shelter, and reading any book within his reach. Hill is a master LEGO builder and constantly on the lookout for materials to rescue from the recycling bin so he can turn them into new creations. Hill was ten years old when he wrote this.

※ ※ ※

How can we pray daily?

Developing a habit of daily prayer is very important to our spiritual health, and there are lots of different ways to pray. The idea of prayer is to have a conversation between you and God, and there's no one right or wrong way to do that. Most people find that their prayer habits develop over time through the changes and chances of life. What works this year might not work next year, and that is fine. But in the same way that you don't stop talking on the phone just because you need a new one, you don't stop talking to God when you need a new practice.

It's a good idea to seek wisdom from a spiritually active friend or a spiritual director or your priest. But you can start praying—or increase the frequency or depth of your prayers—any time.

Pray at mealtimes. Every time you sit down to eat, thank God for the blessings of the meal and any companions who might be with you. Add whatever is on your mind and in your heart. If you're not sure where to start, *The Book of Common Prayer* offers some wonderful prayers for mealtime on page 835.

Simply talk to God. Set aside a time, and perhaps a space, for daily prayer. Some people kneel by their bedside. Others might grab a mug of coffee and a comfy chair. It's up to you. In the morning or in the evening—or any time—just talk to God. Tell God what's on your mind. Say what you're sorry for. Say what you're thankful for. Say those things that you need help with. Say your concerns for the welfare of the world.

Use set forms of prayer. I often prefer to pray using words that have been written out for me, whether in *The Book of Common Prayer* or in other resources. The beautiful language of already-composed prayers sometimes expresses thoughts that I can't quite articulate myself. Also, it is powerful to connect with ancient prayers that are hundreds of years old. You can use very complex or very simple prayers or anything in between. Starting simply is an excellent way to begin. There are lovely one-page prayers for morning, noon, evening, and bedtime in *The Book of Common Prayer* on page 137. You can say these prayers on your own or with other people.

Pray with others. If your church offers prayers during the week, stop by and pray with others. If they don't, maybe pray about whether God is calling you to start a prayer group in your congregation. You can always gather friends or find a church to attend for midweek prayers.

Use tactile prayers. When we pray, our minds may wander. Some people find that prayer beads can help with focus. I like to use traditional rosary beads or Anglican prayer beads, but you can use whatever works. Another way to be tactile is to hold a cross or some other object or perhaps pray while you move. For example, you can pray walking a labyrinth, savoring the feel of your feet touching the ground as you pray along the winding path.

However you pray, find or create a habit of daily prayer. Try it out for a month. At the end of the month, reflect on whether to continue or move in a new direction. I can almost guarantee you will be grateful beyond words.

Paul challenged us to pray without ceasing. That doesn't mean praying every second but rather that our prayers should be regular and ongoing—something we practice throughout the day, each and every day. This life of prayer helps us with the other spiritual practices of the Way of Love, and it will change your life too.

FOR REFLECTION

1. When is a time you prayed in a way that helped you grow in your faith?

2. What keeps you from praying more readily?

3. What might you do to pray in new ways,
   more often?

WRITE IT DOWN

Which of the approaches for praying appeal to you? Write down some ideas for how you might live into this approach. Be specific and realistic for where you are now.

PRAYER

Lord Jesus, who went to the garden to pray, be with me all of my days and help me always to turn to you again and again in prayer. *Amen*.

CHAPTER 4

WORSHIP

Perhaps the most common Christian activity among the Way of Love practices is worship. Worship is offered in majestic cathedrals with soaring music and a congregation of thousands. And worship is offered just as well in small country churches with powerful preaching and a congregation of a dozen. This chapter will not argue for any particular style of worship. You can worship with guitars or organs in churches large or small with solemn formality or intimate informality What we are talking about here is the importance of worship for you and for me and the communities in which we live and love.

When I was a younger adult, I was a bit of a spiritual nomad. I spent several years looking to make sense of the Christian faith. My wandering was all very cerebral. Then one evening, I entered a church with a liturgy that was ceremonially rich and ornate. All of my mental circuit breakers were blown—in a very good way. No one rationalized what happened in Holy Communion. Instead, people genuflected in awe at the majestic presence of Christ in the Blessed Sacrament. There was glorious music and the scent of incense, and all of this was happening in a stunning space. I glimpsed heaven. I was swept along into a realm that was much larger than my imagining. I was with people whose physical postures and actions manifested a sacrificial worship of God in Jesus Christ.

Some years later, I attended a different church that offered morning prayer most days. Just a few people—sometimes one or two or three—would gather to say prayers and read scripture. There was nothing particularly glorious or impressive about this, other than the steadfast faith of a group of people devoted to reading scripture and praying. Again, and in a totally different venue, I glimpsed heaven.

I mention all this because worship, whatever it is and however we do it, can never be about merely following the rules and going through the motions. Whether we are large or small, worshiping with simple or ornate liturgy, when we worship, what we are doing is offering our best to God.

PERSONAL REFLECTION: WORSHIP

I was about sixteen years old and singing in a joint
choir in the Diocese of Texas, and I didn't like the
songs they were singing. Some of them I really,
really didn't like. Like any teenager, I would sing
those with obvious contempt or negativity. I don't
remember the actual event or the specific songs I
didn't like; I just remember seeing pictures from
the event years later and being horrified by my
demeanor.

I am standing there without a smile—and if you
know me, you know that smiling is my favorite. I
have no emotion on my face...I'm just there. I feel
nervous when I think about those pictures because
I have seen many people throughout the years who
look something like that while they are worshiping.
Sometimes they frown, sometimes they look blank.
Sometimes, they are just...there.

In those pictures, I was young, but even then, I
knew what worship meant to me—a way to express
love, gratitude, and commitment to God. Those
pictures look nothing like what my body, soul,

heart, and mind experience when I am worshiping God. As I grow older, every single time I catch myself frowning like my sixteen-year-old self and thinking, "I don't want to sing this song!", I try to remind myself, with the help of the Holy Spirit, "Girl, you're worshiping God. Even with *that* song."

One of my spiritual disciplines is seeking to tell the truth at all times—even when it's hard or uncomfortable for me or others. We read about Jesus and the disciples doing this all the time, so I know I'm in good company, even when the going is rough or disappointing.

God has given me the gift to see and speak into situations some folks don't always know how to see or speak to. As a result, I can often be found criticizing our beloved Episcopal Church on my social media channels. I spend a lot of time talking about our lack of diversity, most often about the lack of diversity in music and music ministries. I believe we should have balance in our worship—a balance between cultural expressions and language and resources.

We are *almost* there with our narrative language and in several liturgical resources, but I often feel we are far from diverse in terms of our music. I often find only one type of hymnal in Episcopal churches and just one or two instruments. As a Latina who loves to just sing loudly and sway to diverse styles of music, I frequently feel let down by the average Sunday musical selections and arrangements.

Yet I also know that I am called to worship God, always, not only when I like the song or when I think it is not diverse enough but always. Don't get me wrong: I am also called to speak truth, but worshiping God comes before, during, and after that—all while smiling broadly, singing loudly, and swaying.

—*Sandra Montes*

Sandra Montes is the interim worship director at Union Seminary and a consultant for the Episcopal Church Foundation. A professional educator with a doctorate in instruction and curriculum, Sandra is a gifted musician and speaker. She loves time with her family, friends, and her companion, La Chank'I the chihuahua.

❋ ❋ ❋

Why worship?

The Episcopal Church is governed by a set of rules called canons. One canon applies to everyone in the church, not just clergy and lay leaders. It reads like this:

> *All persons within this Church shall celebrate and keep the Lord's Day, commonly called Sunday, by regular participation in the public worship of the Church, by hearing the Word of God read and taught, and by other acts of devotion and works of charity, using all godly and sober conversation.* (Title II, Canon 1)

Worship is so important, so central to who we are as a community of faith, that our official rules urge all people—lay and clergy—to practice this step in the Way of Love. Notice what the canon asks us all to do: participate in the public worship of the church and hear the scriptures proclaimed and taught. The canons also urge us to engage in other acts of devotion or charity. All this is to be done on Sunday, which we also call the Lord's Day.

These days, most congregations offer Holy Communion on Sundays. The rules ask us only to hear the Word of God read and taught, which opens up all kinds of worship services, whether or not there is Holy Communion. The important thing for us is to join in public worship. But what is worship, anyway? And how is it different from prayer?

Worship is observing with reverence or prayers and acts of adoration or otherwise showing love and obedience to a deity. In the case of Christian worship, we gather to adore and honor Almighty God, revealed to us as Father, Son, and Holy Spirit. Worshiping means that we recognize the God we worship is greater than we are, which means we are not the center of our worlds. In worship, we make offerings to God—we offer our time, our talents, and some of our stuff to remind ourselves that God is God, and we are not. Out of gratitude for all that God has done for us, we "present our selves, our souls and bodies" before God (*The Book of Common Prayer*, p. 336).

Liturgy

You might hear people say that liturgy means work *of* the people, in the sense that liturgy is about what each person who is present does in the service. But I believe there's much more to it. Liturgy is more like work *for* the people or work for the common good. In ancient Greece, when someone donated money for a public building, the gift was called a liturgy. That is the sense of what we are doing when we worship together. Sure, each person who is present for the service has a role, but what we are doing is bigger than the people in the room. Our liturgy is an act for the good of the world.

Of course, liturgy has another sense. When we Episcopalians gather, we use *The Book of Common Prayer* as an order of service (or guidebook) for all the different ways we pray together. The words we say and the directions we follow are also called the liturgy. We pray out of a book because worship is bigger than the ideas that any one of us might have as individuals. The prayers we say connect us to the practice of Christians throughout time and space, across centuries and continents, beyond language and culture.

So "liturgy" helps us remember that worship is not about us. What we do when we worship as a body is done on behalf of the whole world. That's why it doesn't matter if we worship with twelve people in a country church or thousands of people in a cathedral. In worship, we are always joined to a larger community through time and space.

Our fundamental engagement with worship should not be about our personal preferences but rather what we offer to God. That switches our perspectives, so we don't become consumers or idle critics but rather people who are ready to offer sacrificial worship—giving up our wants and our must-haves and taking up God's.

Our question is never, "What is this worship doing for us?" but rather, "How is this worship helping us offer ourselves to God?" And then, as a follow-up to the second question, we might ask, "How can we offer our best worship to Almighty God?"

How do I worship?

Plenty of books explore great worship, but this book is more about our work in the pews.

There are two pretty obvious and important parts of maintaining the spiritual practice of worship. First, we need to get ourselves to church to join in worship with other followers of Jesus. Second, when we worship, we have to place ourselves in right relation to God and our neighbors.

If we are serious when we say we follow Jesus, worship should be at the top of our list of priorities for how we spend our time. That means we need to get ourselves to church to join a community of disciples who are there to worship God. We need to make space in our schedule. If we have to work on Sunday morning, we need to find a church that offers worship at a different time.

While worship is about God and not us, it is also true that we are radically changed through our worship of God. This is why the steadfast week-in, week-out commitment is important. Some weeks we might not feel like getting ourselves to church, but once we're there, we can draw inspiration from God (of course) and our fellow worshipers. Other weeks, we might be very excited to get to church, and we might be the person who inspires another who is struggling that day. This is the work of community. The struggling and the thriving are all part of it.

If your family includes children, you might want to start your preparation for worship the night before, laying out the clothes your children will wear to church and talking about how important it is to worship God and learn about Jesus. Look for other families who are growing in faith and trying, too. Help each other develop strategies for preparing for worship, and learn what works for your family. Find out what kind of formation your church offers for families. Don't be embarrassed when your kids meltdown very loudly and very publicly. Keep at it and don't lose heart. We learn how to worship by worshiping, and we are all still learning. Church is for everyone.

Once we're at church, the second important aspect of worship takes hold. We come to worship for God. Part of our worship is reminding each other that loving God is the most important thing we do and that being the beloved of God is the most important thing we are. We also practice our love of neighbor as we share God's love for us with our neighbors.

Worship is one of the spiritual practices that encompasses several other practices. In our Holy

Eucharist service, we *turn* when we make our confession, we *learn* when we hear scripture and the sermon, we *pray* throughout the service, we *bless* the world as we make our offerings, we *rest* in the knowledge that God's power working in us can do more than we can ask or imagine, and then, in the end, we are sent out by the dismissal to *go* into the world. If *turn* is the practice that gets us going, *worship* is the glue that holds our spiritual practices together. Worship is one of the ways we keep our hearts and minds alive along the Way of Love—it is one of our most vital practices.

FOR REFLECTION

1. When is a time you worshiped in a way that helped you grow in your faith?

2. What keeps you from worshiping more readily?

3. What might you do to worship in new ways,
    more often?

WRITE IT DOWN

Write down a plan for how you might commit yourself to regular worship. If you attend twice a month, consider weekly services. If you go each Sunday, think about adding a weekday service, maybe even at a different church or in a different style of worship. Be specific and realistic about where are you now and the commitment you might make.

PRAY

Gladden my heart, Almighty God, and give me the desire always to offer in worship my praise and thanks for all that you have done. *Amen*.

CHAPTER 5

BLESS

The steps along the Way of Love don't have to be done in order, and there is some overlap among them. We see this especially in bless and go, which tend to overlap quite a bit. Christians are meant to go out and bless people as we love God and love our neighbors.

In a world that sometimes seems heartless and calculating, we might bless others by being compassionate. In a world that values the accumulation of wealth, we might bless others by giving away our possessions. In a world that often sows confusion, we might bless others by speaking the truth of God's love in Jesus Christ. In other words, there are as many kinds of blessings as there are people to offer them and people to receive them.

Blessing those around us is quite different from merely being nice to them. Being nice means smiling at a hungry person, but offering to buy a meal might be a blessing.

If we're not careful, we might begin to believe that our task is to "help" others. We might convince ourselves of our nobility as we empty our closets and cupboards of things we no longer need to donate to a clothing ministry or a food bank. But the reality is that we're all in need of help, help that only God can give. When I help others, it is God who confers the blessing, and that blessing is conferred on all of us.

Practicing blessing means that we will transgress some of the rules of our culture. Our culture is likely to tell us that other people's problems are not our problems, to hold tight to our possessions and let other people worry about what they need. Our culture is likely to resist the proclamation of truth, preferring us to believe that there is no such thing as truth. Our culture tells us not to talk about our faith outside our churches and families, but we know that Jesus tells us to talk about this good news to the ends of the earth.

How do I bless?

Every person is made in the image of God, and this means that in each person we meet, we are invited to see a reflection of God's glory. When we take this seriously, we will bless others because we will see their inherent dignity and worth. To say that everyone is made in God's image is pretty radical, if you stop and think about it. The people we love are made in God's image. The people who go to our churches are made in God's image. The people we work with are made in God's image. But also, the people we are afraid of are made in God's image. The people who want to hurt us are made in God's image. Whether it's easy for us to glimpse God's glory or difficult to see that reflection, this is our work as followers of Jesus.

Some years ago, I read about a pastor who sent his staff out into the town to observe those around them. He encouraged people to find a park bench or a seat in a coffee shop or a place in the mall. The assignment was to try to watch everyone who passed by with a "God's-eye view," to see people as God sees them. Then the staff met back at the church.

The pastor asked his staff about what they saw. They reported seeing people struggle in big and small ways. They shared about seeing people at the margins of society for one reason or another. But they also reported feeling great love and compassion for these marginalized members of their community. After a long talk, the pastor charged the staff to help change the church and to serve the community outside the church walls—to love all people as God loves them.

This gets to what it means to bless those around us. First, we see. And then, as people of faith, we are compelled and empowered to respond. Perhaps we'll start blessing others by sharing extravagantly of our material goods. Perhaps we'll offer a word of consolation and hope to a stranger in the midst of struggle. Perhaps we'll simply take the time to listen to another human being, to know them for who they are and allow ourselves to be known as well. Perhaps we will be the recipients of blessings and become inspired to offer these gracious gifts to others. In all these ways, we'll be blessed. And in the gracious economy of God, we'll be filled with even more urgency to bless those around us.

PERSONAL REFLECTION: BLESS

We discovered the offering on our porch when we opened the screen door to leave for work. The first blessing came in a five-gallon bucket half full of plump raspberries and a few briars. A couple of weeks later, we received three filets of fish wrapped in butcher paper.

In a village of 254, we lived a thirty-minute drive from the nearest gallon of milk or gas. It wasn't necessarily where we thought we'd begin our life together, but the bishop called my husband to serve the local church. We arrived thinking we would pastor the community; we left knowing they had pastored us.

The blessings continued: a quart jar of just-tapped maple syrup, a bushel of green beans, a loaf of fresh bread. On their own, these gestures might simply be regarded as the hallmarks of a friendly small town. But these gracious gifts shared from the land and larders were only a small part of the blessings bestowed upon us by the flock we loved and tended.

This community knew how to love one another. In the pews gathered all sorts: Billy, who whittled handheld crosses during sermons. Jim slept (and sometimes snored) most Sundays, worn out from his daily two-hour commute. Marie was a bit of a hoarder with a heart for hospitality. Allison wheeled in on her decorated chair, intent that spina bifida was a diagnosis and not a definition.

They loved one another, and they opened their arms to us, strangers bound to flit in and out of their lives in a few short seasons. Faye served juice in jelly jars and shared her love story, even though she had been widowed for decades. Eva exercised her role as the church matriarch through strength of service instead of flexing for power.

Life wasn't perfect there, of course. No place is. Farms and marriages folded. Cancer and age and accidents delivered sucker punches that left us gasping for air and leaning on each other to keep our feet. But in good times and bad, these amazing people continued to thank God for their own blessings and offered blessings to others— sometimes with fruits and vegetables.

May we, inspired by their witness, go and do likewise, extending blessing to all we meet—and receiving them with grateful hearts.

—*Richelle Thompson*

Richelle Thompson lives in Northern Kentucky with her husband and their two teenage children who delight and confound them, often within the same five minutes. They wrangle three dogs, a cat, and a horse and like to spend time camping and laughing with friends and family. Richelle serves as managing editor of Forward Movement and is part of the community of St. Andrew's Episcopal Church, where her husband serves as rector.

※ ※ ※

When we have eyes to glimpse God's glory in others, we will naturally want to bless them. Seeing people who reflect God's glory while living in a refugee camp for years will compel us to work to improve conditions in those places, perhaps even spurring us to work so that they can find permanent homes. Seeing those around us who are not part of a faith community as radiating God's glory will propel us to invite them to know Jesus Christ and thus to find ultimate meaning and holy purpose.

Every blessing we share is the fulfillment of God's promise. In Genesis 12:2, God says to his people, "I will bless you…so that you will be a blessing." The paradox of God's abundant love is that when we seek to be a blessing, we ourselves are blessed. We bless others not out of our own superiority, God forbid, but out of our own humble thanks for all that God has done for us. When we know that we are in need of blessings all the time, we will want to be heralds of God's grace and bearers of God's mercy.

FOR REFLECTION

1. When is a time you blessed or were blessed in a way that helped you grow in your faith?

2. What keeps you from blessing or accepting blessings more readily?

3. What might you do to bless and be blessed in new ways, more often?

WRITE IT DOWN

Which of the approaches for blessing appeal to you?
Write down some ideas for how you might live into
this approach. Be specific and realistic for where you
are now.

PRAY

Christ Jesus, as you have blessed me, help me to be a blessing to others in your name. *Amen.*

CHAPTER 6

GO

In Matthew 28, we find an extraordinary story. Just after his resurrection from the dead, Jesus meets Mary Magdalene and the other Mary near the tomb. He says to them, "Do not be afraid; go and tell my brothers to go to Galilee; there they will see me." Jesus tells the women to go with a message. And that message, in turn, prompts the other disciples to go to Galilee.

Soon after, Jesus meets his disciples on a mountain in Galilee. There, he gives his disciples an instruction— an instruction that continues to be our mission today.

> Go therefore and make disciples of all nations, baptizing them in the name of the Father and of the Son and of the Holy Spirit, and teaching them to obey everything that I have commanded you. And remember, I am with you always, to the end of the age. (Matthew 28:19-20)

The core mission of the disciples, of you and me and everyone we know who calls themselves a Christian, is to go and make disciples. Jesus does not intend for his followers to keep to themselves, to stay in familiar or comfortable places. Thanks be to God, in the centuries after Jesus gave this instruction, those who follow Jesus have gone into the world to make disciples. I am a disciple because someone else made a disciple, and so on all the way back to Jesus.

Jesus himself is always on the move during his ministry. He goes into towns and villages and the countryside to teach people how to live and to offer God's healing love. Jesus clearly has an urgency in his own message and ministry, and he wants his disciples to share in that same sense of urgency.

We see this urgency time and again in scripture. When one of Jesus' followers wants some time to tend to important family matters, the disciple says, "'Lord, first let me go and bury my father.' But Jesus said to him, 'Follow me, and let the dead bury their own dead'" (Matthew 8:21-22). In other words, this mission is too critical to slow down even for family. Another time, one of Jesus' followers says, "'I will follow you, Lord; but let me first say farewell to those at my home.' Jesus said to him, 'No one who puts a hand to the plow and looks back is fit for the kingdom of God'" (Luke 9:61-62). One aspect of go as a spiritual practice is that we have to keep moving, even when that means leaving things behind.

Take some time to read one of the gospels in its entirety in one sitting. It will take you an hour or two, give or take. You'll see a picture of Jesus we don't always glimpse in the sanitized snippets of scripture we hear in the Sunday lectionary. When you binge-read a gospel, you see that Jesus is crystal clear in his focus and goes urgently about his business. We would do well to see that the one we follow and who charges us to go and make disciples isn't asking us to do anything he didn't do himself—he knows exactly what he's asking us to do. And he shows us exactly how to do it.

Go as a practice in church

It's puzzling to me that we sometimes reduce our faith to something that's primarily meant to bring us comfort. It's hard to square the sense of complacency that too often inhabits our churches with the urgency and zeal of Jesus Christ himself. We've all heard people complain about change in the church—and I've done my share of complaining. Isn't it odd though that we complain about something having changed, instead of being upset that things have stayed the same? Our default should be to go, to move, to get on with it. Our savior certainly was always going places and changing things.

PERSONAL REFLECTION: GO

"Do not pass Go, do not collect $200," says the jail card in the game of Monopoly. You can't play if you don't go. Life is like that. You have to go to participate in life.

Go is something that we do each time we leave our homes and interact with others, whether the bus driver or the grocery store clerk. Go is also something that we do each time we reach out on social media to share feelings and stories. In our busy lives, going often becomes routine—whether it involves going out the front door or going online.

We stop paying attention to the ordinary and to others, and going just becomes part of our day.

Yet, even a busy parent accompanying their child to the first day of school walks with intention, arming the child with affirmations of how they will make friends and have fun learning. What if we adopted that kind of intention, of being the face of kindness and appreciation when we go out into the world, encouraging our neighbors the way loving parents encourage a child?

You don't have to go far from home to be an evangelist of good news. This kind of going can begin with relationships within your family, neighborhood, or workplace. The idea is to start where you are. You don't need mobility or foreign language skills. What you need is a humble heart that desires to listen and be present to another's stories of joys and burdens.

When you are out in the world, notice when someone appears to need a word or gesture of kindness. Be the one who says or does something comforting or affirming. Ask: "Would you like a hand with that?" Empathize: "I'm glad we don't have to stand in this line every day." Affirm: "You were patient with that customer." Appreciate: "I count on your helpfulness here." Comfort: "I'm sorry things are so tough right now." Practice communicating with a smile, eye contact, a slight head nod, or touching your heart with your hand.

Go with intention. Pay attention to others. Be kind and affirming.

—*Lelanda Lee*

Lelanda Lee is a member of Saint John's Episcopal Church in Longmont, Colorado. She was a representative from the Episcopal Church's delegation to the fifty-ninth session of the Commission on the Status of Women hosted by the United Nations. She shares her home with her husband Herb and her mother. She and Herb travel anytime and anywhere they can and especially enjoy spending time with their children and grandchildren.

※ ※ ※

Jesus is always reaching out to offer God's healing in sometimes-surprising places to sometimes-shocking people. But on the most important things, he is a constant, abiding teacher. He is consistent in his teaching that we love God and love our neighbors. He is constant in telling the truth always, even when it is dangerous. He is persistent in rejecting the economics and power of empire in favor of the abundance and sacrifice of God's kingdom.

Prayer and worship are the constant, abiding work of the church. Teaching people to love God and love our neighbor is the steady work of the church. Practicing our Anglican ways of praying together is how we live out our corner of the church.

But we need to *go* in how we do church. Maybe that means singing new songs, literally. Maybe it means changing organizational structures. Maybe it means using new technology. Those are the maybes. There are also some musts: We must go into our neighborhoods to learn the needs, hopes, and concerns of the community around us. We must go and listen to the cultures around us so that we might learn how to speak in ways our neighbors can hear and understand. We must go into homes, shopping centers, and sports fields to invite people to join us as followers of Jesus Christ—to go with us.

In particular, we have to go like Jesus. He reaches out to those whom society rejects—notorious sinners, tax collectors, women, children, and so on. In our time, we are meant to go and share God's love with prisoners, migrants, the poor, the desperate, the lonely, and so on. If there is an imaginary line that we might hear ourselves saying, "We should not go there," then it is quite possible Jesus' call is for us to go exactly there.

Following Jesus

In order to go, we first have to see that where we are is not our final destination. We might mean that literally. *Our church community must not be confined to this building. We must go and be the church outside our walls.* Or we might mean this more spiritually. *We can grow more and more into the full stature of Christ, so let us go deeper as followers of Jesus.*

I have said throughout this book that we are followers of Jesus. Being a follower implies movement. I must move to keep up with the leader, and that is easier said than done. To follow someone, I have to trust that they know where they are going or are capable of figuring out how to get there. I have to trust that they will take care to see that I can keep up. I have to trust that the place we are going is a place that will be good for me.

All of this following is somewhat countercultural because following requires me to relinquish control. Being a follower requires me to acknowledge very specifically that I am trusting someone else and putting my well-being in that person's hands. Even the very idea of "following" rather than "leading" is subversive. Bookstores have whole sections devoted to leadership, but we'll probably never see a TED Talk on how to be a good follower.

We follow Jesus. To do this, we must relinquish control. We must trust that he is watching out for us. We must believe that the place he is leading us is far better than the place where we are now. And in order to follow, we have to keep up. We have to *go*.

How can I go?

1. See that we *need* to go. Our whole faith sets us in the context of an earthly pilgrimage in which we are constantly growing into the full stature of Christ. Our faith is meant to grow and deepen over our lives. Our message is meant to be shared with those who do not yet know Jesus. Our calling is to love our neighbors, which explicitly means that we need to know our neighbors and go into the neighborhood, whether we are talking about next-door neighbors or neighbors across the globe.

Read, study, and meditate on Matthew 28, which is all about going.

2. See that Jesus—who is the perfect image of God—was and is always on the move. Read the gospels and take note of all the places he travels, preaching and praising God.

Before Jesus returns to dwell with his Father in heaven, he promises that the Holy Spirit will abide with us, leading us into all truth. This means we don't have to figure out all the answers on our own, and we are never alone. This is important because if you agree with me that we need to move, the natural question will arise: where shall we go?

We can and should pray and work in the community and in our churches to decide which direction to go and how to carry out the mission Jesus has given us. To guard against me coming up with an idea that is not of God, I can pray—and test my idea with others.

Going will likely take us, literally, outside our comfort zones. We'll go into neighborhoods and places that are unfamiliar to us. We'll stretch ourselves through serving others who are not like us at all and through relationships with people who are strangers to us right now. We'll need to find ways to tell the very good news of how Jesus has changed our lives so that the whole world might hear the Good News of God in Jesus Christ.

As a starting place, I suggest going and telling one person about your faith. You don't have to pick a stranger, just someone with whom you usually don't talk about matters of faith. Share with them why Jesus matters to you. Tell them how your part in a community of discipleships sustains you. Explain to them how loving God and loving your neighbor is the most important thing you think you can do with your life. You don't have to convert them or even invite them to church. Just go and tell them about Jesus.

The forces marshalled against us are considerable. Our fears are stoked and the culture of complacency in our church is strong. But the force of Love pushing us outward is stronger than any of the powers in the world. Jesus says again and again, *Be not afraid.* We know that Jesus is the way, the truth, and the life, and we should share him with those who do not yet know him. And of course, as Christians, we can never turn our backs on the needs of our neighbors, across the street or across the ocean. The commandment to love God means we are always growing in faith so that we might more fully love the One who first loved us. The commandment to love our neighbors means that we must know our neighbors and discover ways to share God's love with them. All of this means we have to go. *Go, go, go.* Go, just like Jesus.

FOR REFLECTION

1. When is a time you began to go in a way that helped you grow in your faith?

2. What keeps you from going more readily?

3. What might you do to go in new ways,
   more often?

WRITE IT DOWN

Which of the approaches for going appeal to you?
Write down some ideas for how you might live into
this approach. Be specific and realistic for where you
are now. For instance, if you decide to go and talk
to people about Jesus, name the time, place, and
frequency that you can really do this.

PRAY

As I go forth into the world, O Holy Spirit, guide me to do your will and inspire me with the knowledge that you are always my companion. *Amen*.

CHAPTER 7

REST

How are you? I probably ask and answer this common question a dozen or more times a day. Most often, the response is one word: *busy*.

Our culture values being busy, and we esteem busy people. It's not just adults either. Even preschool-aged children have their playtime carefully scheduled. It's never too soon to start building that resume, whether it's for a job, the perfect college, or even the right kindergarten. We love busy.

And busy is a problem, especially for Christians. I don't think God desires that we run around all the time, not quite keeping up. It's not healthy to be busy all the time. Among other things, studies keep telling us that we're so busy, we're not getting enough sleep. Sleep deprivation is brutal, and besides making folks feel cranky, it can cause all sorts of harmful side effects.

Now it should be noted that some people have no choice but to be overly busy. A person may work a full-time job and a part-time job or two out of necessity, not by choice. And all sorts of family circumstances cause people to stay busy as employees as well as caregivers and so on. Those who have no choice are victims of a culture that values busyness over human flourishing. However, many of us have choices about how much we work and how we spend our time. We can exercise this choice to set aside time for rest, and we can use our choices to change our culture so that rest is possible for all people.

When I was in parish ministry, a parishioner was offered a significant promotion in a corporation. The new job came with an impressive title and a big salary—along with more responsibility and a heavy travel schedule. Many of us would encourage taking the promotion because it was such a good opportunity. But this person turned down the promotion to continue being able to spend time with family—and because the family wanted to be more involved with their church community.

I knew another family with a child in high school who was quite a good athlete. The coach said there would be Sunday practice. Many of us would have said, "We have to be on the sports field and not in church or resting." But this family talked it over and told the coach that practice on Sunday morning was out of the question. (Surprisingly to me, the coach agreed that the child could stay on the team!)

My point is that sometimes *we think* we don't have a choice about staying busy, but we might have more freedom than we imagine. A wise friend explained to me years ago that when we say "yes" to one invitation, we are saying "no" to something else. And when we say "no" to an opportunity, we are leaving room for a "yes" somewhere else.

The pressure to keep busy is enormous, and it comes from every level of society. We are told we need to work more hours to earn more money to fund a certain kind of lifestyle. We are told we need to schedule our children's time so they have the right type of experiences to set them up for success. We are told we need to be available constantly—by phone and by email and by text and whatever new way to communicate has just been invented—so we don't miss anything, so we don't have to say no, so we don't have to turn it off and put it down and rest.

When we rest, we are doing one of the most subversive activities that can be imagined in our consumer-driven culture. Resting means we are rejecting the opportunity to earn money. Resting— if we really, thoroughly rest—means we make ourselves unavailable to the communication demands of the world. Resting means that we value something more than we value all the things that we are told are important.

However, rest is not simply a good nap or setting aside leisure time but a mandate that comes from the wellspring of our faith as disciples of Jesus Christ.

PERSONAL REFLECTION: REST

Practicing a day of rest doesn't seem like it should be as tricky as it is. But resting and honoring the sabbath is as countercultural as following Jesus. We celebrate busyness. While bookstores and checkout lines burgeon with self-care magazines reminding us to breathe, we encourage overscheduling and eschew doing nothing. Otherwise, what will we talk about when we go back to work or wherever we go on Monday mornings?

For me, the hardest part about honoring the sabbath and keeping it holy is giving myself permission to stop. Resting my body, praying, meditating on scripture, and celebrating my many blessings doesn't sound like the reports I have heard on Mondays from colleagues and students. It took me several years to stop doing laundry and other chores on Sunday. I still fight feeling supremely guilty for not pulling weeds in the front yard, but I'm getting there.

What helped me to get to a place where I'm closer to practicing the kind of sabbath that God wants for us—genuine rest to restore our bodies and minds and to spend time in spiritual pursuits—was to slow down during the week. My girls and I had a long commute to get to and from school each day, but I stopped taking the highway and instead chose more beautiful routes. We had to leave earlier, but we enjoyed our beautiful wandering ways so much that when the weekend arrived, we wanted more.

We began hiking as a family. I began to prioritize my physical and mental health. My girls began to see the link between sabbath and self-care. Our family learned to rest well together. And that has made all the difference in how we live together and how we love Jesus and our neighbors.

God shows us how much God loves us by commanding us to honor the sabbath. Permit yourself to honor the God in you by giving yourself the time and space to rest. I'll keep trying; I pray you will, too.

—*Miriam McKenney*

Miriam McKenney is a beloved child of God, wife of David, mother of three, and a long-distance runner. A lifelong lover of books, Miriam has a master's degree in library science. She is the director of development at Forward Movement and a member of the Commission on Ministry for the Diocese of Southern Ohio.

※ ※ ※

God cares about rest

The first chapter of Genesis tells us how God created the heavens, the earth, the sun and moon, the seas, the land, the animals, and finally, people. All this was done in six days. And then:

> Thus, the heavens and the earth were finished, and all their multitude. And on the seventh day God finished the work that he had done, and he rested on the seventh day from all the work that he had done. So God blessed the seventh day and hallowed it, because on it God rested from all the work that he had done in creation. (Genesis 2:1-3)

Almighty God rested. Why would we mortals imagine that we can do just fine without rest? God did not merely rest but set apart and sanctified one day each week for rest. When we also set aside this day for rest, we are honoring God's decision to make rest an integral part of the fabric of creation.

Throughout the first five books of the Bible, there are various regulations concerning this day of rest. In biblical times, profaning the rest day could be a capital offense. The Bible offers several accounts of Jesus keeping the day of rest and teaching people about it. Jesus encourages people to prioritize caring for people or animals in emergencies on the day of rest (and models this on occasion with different healings). Nevertheless, his overall message reinforces the importance of rest and thus honors God's practice and wish that we set this day apart by being still and not treating it like the other six days.

Not only does Jesus consistently keep his day of rest, but he also rests in other ways. He goes away by himself to pray. We might think of his time in the desert as a kind of retreat—a long rest away from distractions. He wants to get away from the chaos and demands of crowds, to be quiet and still. Jesus Christ, God incarnate, needs quiet time and a weekly day to rest. It shouldn't be so hard for us to see that we too need rest and quiet time.

How do we rest?

The first and most obvious thing about resting is that we have to make time for it. If our schedules are totally booked, we have to decide what we're not going to do in order to rest. If you haven't been taking

time for rest, you might start with thirty minutes or
an hour each week and then work your way up to
setting aside the time for rest that God commands.

What does rest look like? Many observant Jews have
various rules about keeping the sabbath, if you want
some guidelines that have been carefully worked out
over centuries. But we are not obligated by those same
rules. You need to work out for yourself what rest
looks like. And also remember: resting in families will
look different than it does for individuals.

I know some people who like to avoid electronic
devices (computers, phones, TVs) when they are
resting. Others may want to sit still and pray or
meditate or just think or, gasp, daydream. One friend
tends to her garden as part of her weekly rest. That
activity—which would feel like work to me—is
rejuvenating for her. My point is that you'll need to
discover exactly what rest looks like, especially if you
haven't been doing it.

All that said, it's important to differentiate between
"not working" and "resting." If I spend my day cleaning
the house and running errands, that's not resting. We

need to take care when we're planning rest to ensure that we are rejuvenated by however we decided to observe that time. It might be better to err on the side of doing less. In our house, we like to have slow days of rest that might include some time at the dog park, a bit of reading together, and maybe a couple of nice meals. Yours will look different.

As with other practices, the spiritual practice of rest takes time to develop. The more we do it, the better we become at embracing rest. Creating space in our lives for rest is especially challenging in our culture, but it is crucial to taking care of the bodies God has given us. It's also keeping a commandment. Rest honors God and helps us be refreshed to carry on with all the other spiritual practices. In other words, it's easier to turn, learn, pray, worship, bless, and go when we're well-rested.

FOR REFLECTION

1. When is a time you rested in a way that helped you grow in your faith?

2. What keeps you from resting?

3. What might you do to rest in new ways,
   more often?

WRITE IT DOWN

Which of the approaches for resting appeal to you?
Write down some ideas for how you might live into
this approach. Be specific and realistic for where
you are now. For instance, if you decide to set aside
sabbath time, name the time, place, and frequency that
you can really do this.

PRAY

Almighty God, as you rested on the seventh day of creation, so help me rest in your presence that I might delight in your works on earth and in heaven. *Amen*.

CHAPTER 8

NEXT STEPS:

DEVELOPING A RULE OF LIFE

We have now worked our way through the Way of Love, a set of seven spiritual practices to help you follow Jesus. It can be hard to know how to integrate all seven practices into our daily lives, so we may find it helpful to craft a rule of life to organize how to develop these spiritual practices.

The term *rule of life* is an ancient one, coming out of the monastic world. Monks and nuns still use rules of life to organize their daily activities of prayer, work, and service. A rule of life helps communities offer their best hospitality. But a rule of life is not just for communities. It can be a helpful tool for individuals as they seek to create patterns of living that help us grow in faith. When we follow a rule of life, the purpose is not so much the rule itself but rather that to which the rule points—our life in Christ.

"Rule" comes from the Latin *regula*. Knowing this helps us remember that the rule of life is meant to regulate our lives. It's easy to say we will pray. But what does that look like? How often will we pray? When we pray, will it be for a few seconds or a few hours? What words will we use? For whom or what will we pray? The rule guides us. For example, my own rule instructs me to pray the Daily Office (Morning Prayer and Evening Prayer from *The Book of Common Prayer*) every day.

Religious communities spend years (if not centuries) refining their community rule of life. Some people who live by a rule of life spend decades developing the rule that will guide them. That can seem daunting. I encourage you to start simply with an achievable rule. You have to start somewhere, and the key is to get moving.

If you don't already have a rule of life, try crafting one. To keep it simple, I suggest you pick three things to work on for one month. If you find that fruitful, then I hope you'll take further steps to develop a deeper, longer-lasting rule of life.

Throughout this book, (I hope) you've been keeping some notes. You have had a chance to reflect on moments when you have practiced the steps of the Way of Love: turn, learn, pray, worship, bless, go, and rest. And you have had some time to think about what keeps you from doing these things. You've even done some thinking about what it might look like to practice them more wholeheartedly. Now, we're ready to get specific, to set and follow a rule of life for one month. Set a rule you can keep, so you'll have a positive feeling of accomplishment, in addition to whatever blessings come your way as you deepen your commitment to follow Jesus.

One month is long enough to form a habit and also long enough to be a bit of a challenge. It's short enough that if you hate the rules you picked, you're only stuck with them for thirty days or so. The point of this exercise is for your own development and well-being, so you can decide to make a rule for a week or a month or a season or whatever length of time you like.

Some of the Way of Love practices are more abstract than others, so set very specific, measurable rules. This helps you recognize if you did the thing you wanted to do or not.

Here are some examples of practices in a rule of life:

- I will give thanks in prayer every time I eat.

- I will read one whole book of the Bible.

- I will make sure I'm in church every Sunday and attend one midweek service each week.

- I will serve in a feeding ministry once a week.

- I will stay away from the phone and all electronic devices for one half day every week.

- I will find a way to bless one person in my social media circles with kindness every day.

- I will look up the scripture readings and spend some time reading them before church.

- I will spend ten minutes praying for the needs of my community every day.

These are just a few ideas to help you decide what you will do. I suggest that you choose three rules to begin practicing at first. Think of three things you can realistically do, and maybe even push yourself a bit.

This is not meant to add to your already overbooked to-do list. A rule of life, when lived, will eventually organize your entire life to help you be more focused on following Jesus. The people I know who faithfully keep a robust rule of life are often filled with the peace that passes all understanding precisely because their first priority is being a disciple of Jesus. This is a fruit of a faith that is fully alive.

Before you start jotting down ideas, set aside some time—maybe an hour—for reflection. Begin in prayer, asking God to help you know how to live as a follower of Jesus. Ask God to give you wisdom and understanding. Ask God for clarity. Then, be still and listen.

Part of listening might be a little time re-reading the notes you've made in previous chapters—especially the notes from the Write It Down sections. What calls out to you? Jot down a few ideas. Pray some more. Try to decide on three rules. How do you know which rules to establish? Prayer will surely help. You might also talk with your priest or a wise spiritual friend about your rule and how you intend to apply it. Get feedback from them. When you feel ready, write down your three rules.

Try these for a month. Mark your calendar or set a reminder on your device to check in with yourself after thirty days. If you realize you didn't quite get it right, you can adjust or try it again. If you fail to keep your rule, remember the first spiritual practice of the Way of Love: turn! Jesus loves you whether you keep the rule or fail, and he will welcome you when you try again. These practices are meant to be used in our whole lives, every day, year after year. In order to live this way, we need a rule of life to keep us going in the Way of Love. These rules will not be a burden. The rules of the Way of Love will be a compass.

So, to summarize, these are the steps to create your trial rule of life.

1. Spend time in prayer and reflection on what you wrote as you read this book.

2. Write down your three rules and try them for a month.

3. After a month, spend time revisiting your three
    rules by praying and reflecting. If you need to,
    modify your three rules or try different rules, and
    give it another try.

When you're ready to think about developing a
lasting rule of life, you might talk with your priest or
a spiritual director. Many religious communities of
monks and nuns offer retreats, and you might go on
retreat to spend time reflecting on a rule of life—your
own or one that is practiced by a particular order.
And, yes, there are monks and nuns in the Episcopal
Church! For example, the Society of St. John the
Evangelist is an order of monks based in Cambridge,
Massachusetts. They even offer a free six-week set of
reflections to help you craft a rule of life (See details
in the Appendix, Resource section).

The point of a rule of life is to keep us real.
Sometimes we rebel against rules. We might think
that, as Christians, rules are for other people. But the
truth is, we all need rules. Jesus tells us to love our
neighbors. If we don't have rules, there's a risk we'll
interpret "love your neighbor" to mean "be nice to
people who look like me." But Jesus also gives us some

rules about how to love our neighbor. He teaches us that everyone is our neighbor. He tells us to love our enemies. He gives us examples that include welcoming strangers, visiting prisoners, and clothing the naked.

The Way of Love, without any practical applications or rules or instructions, is the sort of thing that we might read about and feel vaguely happy things. Oh, that's nice. But the key to taking our journey seriously as followers of Jesus is to create a rule of life to help us live out these spiritual practices. There's no one way to do this. That's why it's up to you to decide—with God's help—how you will follow Jesus along with this Way of Love.

The Way of Love invites us all to turn, learn, pray, worship, bless, go, and rest. May you be blessed in your journey. Remember that God the Father sent Jesus Christ into this world in great love, and we have been promised the companionship of the Holy Spirit. You are never alone in this joyous, holy, and life-giving work.

Go in the Way of Love.

FOR REFLECTION

What are some ideas for your rule of life? Jot down a
few possible rules.

After you have done some more praying and perhaps
spoken with others, what rule of life will you keep for
one month? Write down three rules:

1.

2.

3.

APPENDIX

The Way of Love may be new, but the seven practices are as ancient as the scriptures. Some of the following readings are mentioned in the chapters on each practice, while others simply illustrate how the spiritual practices of the Way of Love are found in the Bible. You may like to read through these verses to learn more, or you may want to spend time meditating on the passages.

These readings would be excellent material for a Bible study in a Way of Love class. Whether you are reading devotionally or for a group study, here are three ways to reflect on each reading. 1. Retell the story. What does the text say about the practice? 2. Notice places in the text that stand out to you. What inspires or delights or amuses or outrages you? 3. Connect the reading with your life. How does this reading about a particular spiritual practice connect with your life?

READINGS

Chapter 1: Turn

Exodus 3:1-15

Moses was keeping the flock of his father-in-law Jethro, the priest of Midian; he led his flock beyond the wilderness, and came to Horeb, the mountain of God. There the angel of the Lord appeared to him in a flame of fire out of a bush; he looked, and the bush was blazing, yet it was not consumed. Then Moses said, "I must turn aside and look at this great sight, and see why the bush is not burned up." When the Lord saw that he had turned aside to see, God called to him out of the bush, "Moses, Moses!" And he said, "Here I am." Then he said, "Come no closer! Remove the sandals from your feet, for the place on which you are standing is holy ground." He said further, "I am the God of your father, the God of Abraham, the God of Isaac, and the God of Jacob." And Moses hid his face, for he was afraid to look at God.

Then the Lord said, "I have observed the misery of my people who are in Egypt; I have heard their cry on account of their taskmasters. Indeed, I know their sufferings, and I have come down to deliver them from the Egyptians, and to bring them up out of that land to a good and broad land, a land flowing with milk and honey, to the country of the Canaanites, the Hittites, the Amorites, the Perizzites, the Hivites, and the Jebusites. The cry of the Israelites has now come to me; I have also seen how the Egyptians oppress them. So come, I will send you to Pharaoh to bring my people, the Israelites, out of Egypt." But Moses said to God, "Who am I that I should go to Pharaoh, and bring the Israelites out of Egypt?" He said, "I will be with you; and this shall be the sign for you that it is I who sent you: when you have brought the people out of Egypt, you shall worship God on this mountain."

But Moses said to God, "If I come to the Israelites and say to them, 'The God of your ancestors has sent me to you,' and they ask me, 'What is his name?' what shall I say to them?" God said to Moses, "I am who I am." He said further, "Thus you shall say to the Israelites, 'I am has sent me to you.'" God also said to Moses, "Thus you shall say to the Israelites, 'The Lord, the God of your ancestors, the God of Abraham, the God of Isaac, and the God of Jacob, has sent me to you': This is my name forever, and this my title for all generations."

Matthew 4:17

From that time Jesus began to proclaim, "Repent, for the kingdom of heaven has come near."

Acts 2:37-42

Now when they heard this, they were cut to the heart and said to Peter and to the other apostles, "Brothers, what should we do?" Peter said to them, "Repent, and be baptized every one of you in the name of Jesus Christ so that your sins may be forgiven; and you will receive the gift of the Holy Spirit. For the promise is for you, for your children, and for all who are far away, everyone whom the Lord our God calls to him." And he testified with many other arguments and exhorted them, saying, "Save yourselves from this corrupt generation." So those who welcomed his message were baptized, and that day about three thousand persons were added. They devoted themselves to the apostles' teaching and fellowship, to the breaking of bread and the prayers.

Chapter 2: Learn

Deuteronomy 11:18-21

You shall put these words of mine in your heart and soul, and you shall bind them as a sign on your hand, and fix them as an emblem on your forehead. Teach them to your children, talking about them when you are at home and when you are away, when you lie down and when you rise. Write them on the doorposts of your house and on your gates, so that your days and the days of your children may be multiplied in the land that the LORD swore to your ancestors to give them, as long as the heavens are above the earth.

Romans 12:1-12

I appeal to you therefore, brothers and sisters, by the mercies of God, to present your bodies as a living sacrifice, holy and acceptable to God, which is your spiritual worship. Do not be conformed to this world, but be transformed by the renewing of your minds, so that you may discern what is the will of God—what is good and acceptable and perfect.

For by the grace given me I say to everyone among you not to think of yourself more highly than you ought to think, but to think with sober judgement, each according to the measure of faith God has assigned. For as in one body we have many members, and not all the members have the same function, so we, who are many, are one body in Christ, and individually we are members one of another. We have gifts that differ according to the grace given to us: prophecy, in proportion to faith; ministry, in ministering; the teacher in teaching; the exhorter, in exhortation; the giver, in generosity; the leader, in diligence; the compassionate in cheerfulness.

Let love be genuine; hate what is evil, hold fast to what is good; love one another with mutual affection; outdo one another in showing honor. Do not lag in zeal, be ardent in spirit, serve the Lord. Rejoice in hope, be patient in suffering, persevere in prayer.

Philippians 4:8-9

Finally, beloved, whatever is true, whatever is honorable, whatever is just, whatever is pure, whatever is pleasing, whatever is commendable, if there is any excellence and if there is anything worthy of praise, think about these things. Keep on doing the things that you have learned and received and heard and seen in me, and the God of peace will be with you.

Chapter 3: Pray

Matthew 6:5-15

And whenever you pray, do not be like the hypocrites; for they love to stand and pray in the synagogues and at the street corners, so that they may be seen by others. Truly I tell you, they have received their reward. But whenever you pray, go into your room and shut the door and pray to your Father who is in secret; and your Father who sees in secret will reward you.

"When you are praying, do not heap up empty phrases as the Gentiles do; for they think that they will be heard because of their many words. Do not be like them, for your Father knows what you need before you ask him.

"Pray then in this way:
Our Father in heaven,
hallowed be your name.

Your kingdom come.
Your will be done,
on earth as it is in heaven.

Give us this day our daily bread.

And forgive us our debts,
as we also have forgiven our debtors.

And do not bring us to the time of trial,
but rescue us from the evil one.

For if you forgive others their trespasses, your heavenly Father will also forgive you; but if you do not forgive others, neither will your Father forgive your trespasses."

Colossians 4:2-4

Devote yourselves to prayer, keeping alert in it with thanksgiving. At the same time pray for us as well that God will open to us a door for the word, that we may declare the mystery of Christ, for which I am in prison, so that I may reveal it clearly, as I should.

1 Thessalonians 5:12-22

But we appeal to you, brothers and sisters, to respect those who labor among you, and have charge of you in the Lord and admonish you; esteem them very highly in love because of their work. Be at peace among yourselves. And we urge you, beloved, to admonish the idlers, encourage the fainthearted, help the weak, be patient with all of them. See that none of you repays evil for evil, but always seek to do good to one another and to all. Rejoice always, pray without ceasing, give thanks in all circumstances; for this is the will of God in Christ Jesus for you. Do not quench the Spirit. Do not despise the words of prophets, but test everything; hold fast to what is good; abstain from every form of evil.

Chapter 4: Worship

Deuteronomy 5:6-11

I am the LORD your God, who brought you out of the land of Egypt, out of the house of slavery; you shall have no other gods before me.

You shall not make for yourself an idol, whether in the form of anything that is in heaven above, or that is on the earth beneath, or that is in the water under the earth. You shall not bow down to them or worship them; for I the

LORD your God am a jealous God, punishing children for the iniquity of parents, to the third and fourth generation of those who reject me, but showing steadfast love to the thousandth generation of those who love me and keep my commandments.

You shall not make wrongful use of the name of the LORD your God, for the LORD will not acquit anyone who misuses his name.

Matthew 4:23

Jesus went throughout Galilee, teaching in their synagogues and proclaiming the good news of the kingdom and curing every disease and every sickness among the people.

Hebrews 10:23-25

Let us hold fast to the confession of our hope without wavering, for he who has promised is faithful. And let us consider how to provoke one another to love and good deeds, not neglecting to meet together, as is the habit of some, but encouraging one another, and all the more as you see the Day approaching.

Chapter 5: Bless

Genesis 12:2

I will make of you a great nation, and I will bless you, and make your name great, so that you will be a blessing.

Numbers 6:22-27

The LORD spoke to Moses, saying: Speak to Aaron and his sons, saying, Thus you shall bless the Israelites: You shall say to them,
The LORD bless you and keep you;
    the LORD make his face to shine upon you,
        and be gracious to you;
    the LORD lift up his countenance upon you,
        and give you peace.
So they shall put my name on the Israelites,
        and I will bless them.

Matthew 5:1-11

When Jesus saw the crowds, he went up the mountain; and after he sat down, his disciples came to him. Then he began to speak, and taught them, saying:
"Blessed are the poor in spirit, for theirs is the kingdom
    of heaven.
"Blessed are those who mourn, for they will be comforted.

"Blessed are the meek, for they will inherit the earth.
"Blessed are those who hunger and thirst for righteousness,
    for they will be filled.
"Blessed are the merciful, for they will receive mercy.
"Blessed are the pure in heart, for they will see God.
"Blessed are the peacemakers, for they will be called
    children of God.
"Blessed are those who are persecuted for
    righteousness' sake,
    for theirs is the kingdom of heaven.
"Blessed are you when people revile you and persecute you
    and utter all kinds of evil against you falsely on
    my account."

Chapter 6: Go

Psalm 121:7-8

The LORD shall preserve you from all evil; it is he who shall
keep you safe. The LORD shall watch over your going out
and your coming in, from this time forth for evermore.

Matthew 28

After the sabbath, as the first day of the week was dawning,
Mary Magdalene and the other Mary went to see the tomb.
And suddenly there was a great earthquake; for an angel of

the Lord, descending from heaven, came and rolled back the stone and sat on it. His appearance was like lightning, and his clothing white as snow. For fear of him the guards shook and became like dead men. But the angel said to the women, "Do not be afraid; I know that you are looking for Jesus who was crucified. He is not here; for he has been raised, as he said. Come, see the place where he lay. Then go quickly and tell his disciples, 'He has been raised from the dead, and indeed he is going ahead of you to Galilee; there you will see him.' This is my message for you." So they left the tomb quickly with fear and great joy, and ran to tell his disciples. Suddenly Jesus met them and said, "Greetings!" And they came to him, took hold of his feet, and worshiped him. Then Jesus said to them, "Do not be afraid; go and tell my brothers to go to Galilee; there they will see me."

While they were going, some of the guard went into the city and told the chief priests everything that had happened. After the priests had assembled with the elders, they devised a plan to give a large sum of money to the soldiers, telling them, "You must say, 'His disciples came by night and stole him away while we were asleep.' If this comes to the governor's ears, we will satisfy him and keep you out of trouble." So they took the money and did as they were directed. And this story is still told among the Jews to this day.

Now the eleven disciples went to Galilee, to the mountain to which Jesus had directed them. When they saw him, they worshiped him; but some doubted. And Jesus came and said to them, "All authority in heaven and on earth has been given to me. Go therefore and make disciples of all nations, baptizing them in the name of the Father and of the Son and of the Holy Spirit, and teaching them to obey everything that I have commanded you. And remember, I am with you always, to the end of the age."

Luke 10:1-11

After this the Lord appointed seventy others and sent them on ahead of him in pairs to every town and place where he himself intended to go. He said to them, "The harvest is plentiful, but the laborers are few; therefore ask the Lord of the harvest to send out laborers into his harvest. Go on your way. See, I am sending you out like lambs into the midst of wolves. Carry no purse, no bag, no sandals; and greet no one on the road. Whatever house you enter, first say, 'Peace to this house!' And if anyone is there who shares in peace, your peace will rest on that person; but if not, it will return to you. Remain in the same house, eating and drinking whatever they provide, for the laborer deserves to be paid. Do not move about from house to house. Whenever you enter a town and its people welcome you, eat what is set before you; cure the sick who are there, and

say to them, 'The kingdom of God has come near to you.'
But whenever you enter a town and they do not welcome
you, go out into its streets and say, 'Even the dust of your
town that clings to our feet, we wipe off in protest against
you. Yet know this: the kingdom of God has come near.'"

Chapter 7: Rest

Genesis 2:2-3

And on the seventh day God finished the work that he had
done, and he rested on the seventh day from all the work
that he had done. So God blessed the seventh day and
hallowed it, because on it God rested from all the work
that he had done in creation.

Deuteronomy 5:12-15

Observe the sabbath day and keep it holy, as the LORD your
God commanded you. Six days you shall labor and do all
your work. But the seventh day is a sabbath to the LORD
your God; you shall not do any work—you, or your son
or your daughter, or your male or female slave, or your ox
or your donkey, or any of your livestock, or the resident
alien in your towns, so that your male and female slave
may rest as well as you. Remember that you were a slave in

the land of Egypt, and the L<small>ORD</small> your God brought you out from there with a mighty hand and an outstretched arm; therefore the L<small>ORD</small> your God commanded you to keep the sabbath day.

Matthew 6:30–32

But if God so clothes the grass of the field, which is alive today and tomorrow is thrown into the oven, will he not much more clothe you—you of little faith? Therefore do not worry, saying, "What will we eat?" or "What will we drink?" or "What will we wear?" For it is the Gentiles who strive for all these things; and indeed your heavenly Father knows that you need all these things.

RESOURCES

Websites

The Way of Love: episcopalchurch.org/way-of-love

Intentional Small Group: episcopalchurch.org/way-of-love/intentional-small-group-resources

Becoming Beloved Community: episcopalchurch.org/beloved-community

Books

The Way of Love Bible Challenge edited by Marek Zabreskie. Forward Movement, 2019

The Very Best Day: The Way of Love for Children by Roger Hutchison. Church Publishing, 2020

Videos

Explore the Way of Love: episcopalchurch.org/way-of-love/explore

Traveling the Way of Love: episcopalchurch.org/traveling-the-way-love

Podcasts

Way of Love with Bishop Curry: wayoflove.episcopalchurch.org

Walking Together in the Way of Love: podcasts.apple.com/us/podcast/walking-together-in-the-way-of-love/id1466279770

Experiencing Jesus: experiencingjesuswithbishopmariann.simplecast.fm

Turn

The Disciple's Way by Gilbert Symons. Forward Movement, 1934, rev.
ed. 2012

Joy in Confession: Reclaiming Sacramental Reconciliation by Hillary D.
Raining. Forward Movement, 2017

Learn

The Path: A Journey through the Bible. Forward Movement, 2016

The Bible Challenge edited by Marek Zabreskie. Forward Movement, 2012

Also available: 40 Day Bible Challenges for Matthew, Mark, Luke,
John, and Acts

Pray

Daily Prayer: prayer.forwardmovement.org

Read *Forward Day by Day*, includes scripture and reflections.
Available in print, online, as an app, and a podcast

Saint Augustine's Prayer Book, rev. ed. Forward Movement, 2014

Hour by Hour. Forward Movement, 2012 (Brief versions of the Daily
Office)

Worship

Gifts of God for the People of God: Exploring Worship in the Episcopal Church
by Furman L. Buchanan. Forward Movement, 2019

Inwardly Digest: The Prayer Book as Guide to a Spiritual Life by Derek
Olsen. Forward Movement, 2016

Walk in Love: Episcopal Beliefs and Practices by Scott Gunn and Melody
Shobe. Forward Movement, 2018

Bless

The Dream of God: A Call to Return by Verna J. Dozier. Church
    Publishing, 2006
Episcopal Relief & Development: episcopalrelief.org

Go

The Social Justice Bible Challenge, edited by Marek Zabreskie. Forward
    Movement, 2017
Crazy Christians: A Call to Follow Jesus by Michael B. Curry. Church
    Publishing, 2013

Rest

Sabbath as Resistance: Saying No to the Culture of Now by Walter
    Brueggemann. Westminster/John Knox Press, 2017
Simpler Living, Compassionate Life: A Christian Perspective edited by
    Michael Schut. Church Publishing, 2009

Rule of Life

Living Intentionally: A Workbook for Creating a Personal Rule of Life. SSJE.
    ssje.org/2012/02/20/the-rule-of-the-society-of-saint-john-
    the-evangelist-2
The Restoration Project by Christopher Martin. Forward Movement,
    2014

ABOUT THE AUTHOR

Scott Gunn is the executive director of Forward Movement, a ministry of the Episcopal Church that inspires disciples and empowers evangelists. Scott travels widely as a speaker, retreat leader, and preacher. He is the author of the best-selling *Walk in Love: Episcopal Beliefs & Practices* and *Faithful Questions: Exploring the Way with Jesus.* Before his work at Forward Movement, Scott was a parish priest in Rhode Island. He has worked in technology at nonprofits, a media company, and a university. He is also one of George T. Dog's humans.

ABOUT FORWARD MOVEMENT

Forward Movement inspires disciples and empowers evangelists. While we produce great resources like this book, Forward Movement is not a publishing company. We are a discipleship ministry. Publishing books, daily reflections, studies for small groups, and online resources are important ways we live out this ministry. People around the world read daily devotions through *Forward Day by Day*, which is also available in Spanish (*Adelante Dia a Dia*) and Braille, online, as a podcast, and as an app for your smartphone. We actively seek partners across the church and look for ways to provide resources that inspire and challenge. A ministry of the Episcopal Church since 1935, Forward Movement is a nonprofit organization funded by sales of resources and gifts from generous donors.

To learn more about Forward Movement and our work, visit us at forwardmovement.org or venadelante.org. We are delighted to be doing this work and invite your prayers and support.